SKATEBOARD
VERT

BY THOMAS STREISSGUTH

TORQUE

BELLWETHER MEDIA · MINNEAPOLIS, MN

Are you ready to take it to the extreme? Torque books thrust you into the action-packed world of sports, vehicles, and adventure. These books may include dirt, smoke, fire, and dangerous stunts. WARNING: Read at your own risk.

This edition first published in 2008 by Bellwether Media.

No part of this publication may be reproduced in whole or in part without written permission of the publisher. For information regarding permission, write to Bellwether Media Inc., Attention: Permissions Department, Post Office Box 19349, Minneapolis, MN 55419.

Library of Congress Cataloging-in-Publication Data
Streissguth, Thomas, 1958–
  Skateboard vert / by Thomas Streissguth.
    p. cm. — (Torque : action sports)
  Summary: "Amazing photography accompanies engaging information about Skateboard Vert. The combination of high-interest subject matter and light text is intended for students in grades 3 through 7"—Provided by publisher.
  Includes bibliographical references and index.
  ISBN-13: 978-1-60014-141-6 (hardcover : alk. paper)
  ISBN-10: 1-60014-141-2 (hardcover : alk. paper)
  1. Skateboarding—Juvenile literature. I. Title.

  GV859.8.S863 2008
  796.22—dc22   2007041382

CONTENTS

WHAT IS VERT SKATEBOARDING?

Vert skateboarders seem to defy **gravity**. The word *vert* stands for *vertical*. Vert skaters ride up and down ramps. They perform daring stunts on the top edge of a ramp or in the air above the edge. Then they land on the ramp and cruise back down.

The vertical surface is a key part of the sport. Vert skateboarding started in the 1960s when skaters discovered that empty swimming pools were great places to do tricks. Vert skateboarding started in California.

Wooden ramps became popular in the 1970s. U-shaped ramps, called **half-pipes**, were specially designed for skateboarding. Most half-pipes have walls between 8 and 12 feet (2.4 and 3.7 meters) high.

EQUIPMENT AND FEATURES

The skateboard has a simple design. Skaters stand on the wooden **deck**. Vert skaters use bigger decks than street skaters. The bigger deck gives the skater more control when doing tricks. **Trucks** connect the wheels to the deck. The wheels are made of a hard plastic called **urethane**. **Bearings** help the wheels move smoothly.

Vert riders use special skating shoes. Groove patterns in the soles help the shoes stick to the deck. **Grip tape** on top of the deck also helps a skater stay on the board.

Vert skater Bob Burnquist pulled off an incredible jump in 2006. He skated a 40-foot (12.2-meter) ramp set up at the Grand Canyon in Arizona. He flew out of the ramp and onto a 40-foot (12.2-meter) rail. He slid to the end of the rail and dropped 1,600 feet (487.7 meters) into the Grand Canyon. Wearing a parachute, he landed safely at the bottom.

Safety equipment
is essential to protect the
skater in case of a fall.
Vert skaters always wear
helmets. They also wear
elbow and knee pads.

A half-pipe has several important features. A steel edge called **coping** runs along the top. Skaters "get air" any time they fly above the coping. The curve at the bottom of the ramp is called the **transition**. Skaters gain speed on their way down the transition. They can use this speed for their next trick.

VERT SKATEBOARDING IN ACTION

Vert skaters practice many different moves. In the **axle stall**, the skater rides to the top of the ramp and freezes for a few seconds. His trucks balance on the coping.

Turns and spins in the air are common. Making a full spin in the air is a 360. Making two full spins is a 720. The amazing Tony Hawk is the first skater to land a 900. A 900 is two and a half spins in the air!

Tony Hawk did the first 900 in a timed competition at the 1999 X Games. Unfortunately, he did the move after his time was up. The judges couldn't count it.

Skateboarders can find many opportunities to compete. The most famous vert competition takes place at the ESPN X Games. Since 2004, the X Games have featured an extreme form of the sport called big air skateboarding. This event uses an incredible 80-foot (24.4-meter) megaramp. Riders perform big tricks over a huge 70-foot (21.3-meter) gap. The best riders can make even these tricks look easy.

GLOSSARY

axle stall—a trick in which a skater freezes for a moment on the coping at the top of a half-pipe ramp

bearings—metal parts that make wheels move smoothly

coping—the metal rail at the top of a half-pipe

deck—the wooden riding surface of a skatebaord

gravity—the force that pulls all objects or bodies downward, toward the Earth

grip tape—a sticky tape put on the top of the deck; grip tape helps the skater keep his or her shoes on the board.

half-pipes—ramps with steep walls; half-pipes are shaped like half of a round pipe.

transition—the curved area at the bottom of a half-pipe wall

trucks—the part of the skateboard that connects the wheels to the deck

urethane—a durable material used to make skateboard wheels

TO LEARN MORE

AT THE LIBRARY

Braun, Eric. *Tony Hawk*. Minneapolis, Minn.: Lerner, 2004.

David, Jack. *Big Air Skateboarding*. Minneapolis, Minn.: Bellwether, 2008.

Hocking, Justin. *Skateboarding Tricks and Techniques*. New York: PowerKids Press, 2006.

Streissguth, Thomas. *Skateboarding Street Style*. Minneapolis, Minn.: Bellwether, 2008.

ON THE WEB

Learning more about skateboard vert is as easy as 1, 2, 3.

1. Go to www.factsurfer.com
2. Enter "skateboard vert" into search box.
3. Click the "Surf" button and you will see a list of related web sites.

With factsurfer.com, finding more information is just a click away.

INDEX

The images in this book are reproduced through the courtesy of: ESPN Images, front cover, pp. 6, 7, 14; Eric Lars Bakke, pp. 4, 5, 10, 12; Scott Clarke, pp. 7, 9 (bottom); Markus Paulsen, p. 11; Bryce Kanights, pp. 15 (right), 20; Juan Martinez, p. 17; Getty Images, pp. 6, 9 (top), 15 (left), 18, 19; Tony Vu, p. 21.